As darkness fell on the small house on the eastern slope of the Urals, the band of Bolsheviks stood inside before the deposed Tsar. Nicholas rose from his chair and clung to Alexandra, trying in vain to protect her. One of the executioners pointed a pistol at the Tsar's head and fired. In terror, Alexandra made the sign of the cross before she, too, was killed with a single shot...

Strangely, this moment of tragedy was the culmination of a love story.

HEIRS TO AN EMPIRE

WHEN THEY FIRST MET, HE GAVE HER A BROOCH. SHE, A GRANDDAUGHTER OF QUEEN VICTORIA, WAS JUST 12. HE WAS LITTLE MORE THAN A BOY YET, IN ONE BRIEF MOMENT, THE DESTINY OF THE LAST OF THE TSARS WAS SET

IN A VAST LAND OF ROLLING GRASSY PLAINS, great rivers and endless pine forests covered in snow, in a country of 130 million people of many different races, languages and customs, a Prince was born into the Royal House of Romanov on 18 May 1868.

As grandson of a Tsar and son of the future Tsar, this chubby baby boy seemed, at the time, to be the very epitome of a child born with the world at his feet – a life of privilege lay before him. But history had reserved a more tragic role for him.

Russia, a century ago, was a great empire stretching from the Baltic Sea in the west to the Pacific Ocean in the east, its entire destiny controlled by one man – the Tsar. The Tsar's power was absolute. He spent most of his time in the great capital cities of Moscow and St Petersburg, with their fabulous palaces and ornately decorated churches, home of the religious leaders, the long-bearded priests of the Russian Orthodox Church.

A Tsar is born

But the fantastic, glittering court of the Romanovs and the sumptuous pomp and pageantry of the church was a long way from life in the Russian villages. 'It is very far to the Tsar,' ran an old Russian proverb, and for the millions of simple peasants who were his subjects, life had hardly changed during the 400 years since the days of the first 'Tsar of All the Russias', Ivan the Terrible.

However, by the end of the 19th century, there were rumblings in the empire. The coming of the railroads had opened up the previously scattered and isolated towns and villages to trade and travel, while in the cities people were becoming better educated. There were growing demands that the Voice of the People be heard.

Yet who, of the glittering array of courtiers

The Image Bank/Rentmeester

Hulton-Deutsch Collection

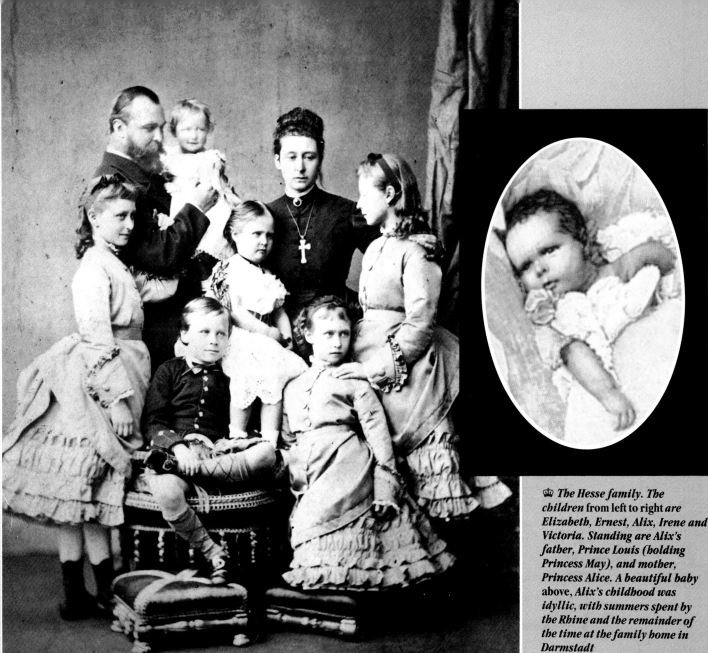

Hulton-Deutsch Collection

Mary Evans Picture Library

♔ *The Hesse family. The children* from left to right *are Elizabeth, Ernest, Alix, Irene and Victoria. Standing are Alix's father, Prince Louis (holding Princess May), and mother, Princess Alice. A beautiful baby above, Alix's childhood was idyllic, with summers spent by the Rhine and the remainder of the time at the family home in Darmstadt*

♔ *Nicholas enjoyed a close relationship with his mother Marie Fedorovna, as can be seen in this picture* left, *taken in 1870, with Nicholas aged two. An immensely popular woman, Marie would always prove a natural ally, acting as a buffer between the shy Tsarevich and his rather gruff, stern father*

and prominent nobility that attended the christening, would have predicted that the baby, Nicholas Alexandrovich, was destined to be the last Tsar of Imperial Russia?

Life at Gatchina

Nicholas's early years were dominated by the larger-than-life personality of his father, Alexander III, who dominated his children as he was one day to dominate Russia. Huge and bearlike at six feet four inches tall, he was an enormously strong man who could bend iron bars with his bare hands. He subjected his children to a disciplined regime, and extended this particularly to Nicholas, to toughen him up for his future role as supreme ruler of all Russia.

Life at Gatchina was strict. In the morning, Nicholas's father would rise at seven and have an ice-cold bath, and his young son was expected to follow suit. Next came a simple peasant breakfast of porridge, boiled eggs and rye bread. At lunchtime, the children were always served last. Sometimes, there would be nothing left

and Nicholas, the future Tsar, would go hungry.

For all his father's efforts, Nicholas grew up a gentle, good-natured child, greatly enjoying the company and friendship of his younger brother George. His mother, Marie, was another natural ally. A gay, fun-loving woman, who relished the hectic social life of the St Petersburg aristocracy, she was also an extremely devoted mother, and was especially protective of her shy son.

Birth of a Princess

While Nicholas was growing up in the bewildering complex of a palatial home near St Petersburg, in the sleepy old town of Darmstadt in Germany, inside a Grand Duke's Palace surrounded by cobblestoned streets and chestnut trees, a little Princess cast sunshine all around her. Her father, Prince Louis, was Grand Duke of the Province of Hesse; her mother, Princess Alice, was the second daughter of Queen Victoria. Born on 6 June 1872, she was christened, on her parents' wedding anniversary, Victoria Alix Helena Louise Beatrice. She was called Princess Alix, but will always be remembered as Alexandra, the last Empress of Russia.

By all accounts, the little Princess was an exceptionally beautiful baby. Her mother, Princess Alice, wrote to Queen Victoria: 'Baby is like [her sister] Ella, only with smaller features, and still darker eyes, with very black lashes, and reddish brown hair. She is a sweet, merry little person, always laughing.'

A baby dies

This was a warm and loving family, but one which was soon to suffer tragedy. One day in 1873, while Alice watched helpless and horrified, her baby boy, Prince Frederick, fell to his death from an upstairs window. The grief-stricken Alice somehow pulled herself together for the sake of the other children. Besides, she had her darling baby daughter, whom she nicknamed Sunny, for her smile. 'Sunny in pink is immensely admired,' she wrote to Victoria.

Alix, the Sunny Princess, spent most of her babyhood in the nursery of the house, known as the New Palace, in Darmstadt.

The nursery at Darmstadt was ruled by 'Orchie', Mrs Orchard, the classic Victorian English nanny – kind but firm. Life in the nursery, and later in the schoolroom, followed strict and very English rules, on the same lines as those laid down by Queen Victoria for her own nine children. Modesty in all things was the order of the day. Little Princess Alix's mother and father both gave away a

_{By gracious permission of HM the Queen}

great deal of their money to charity and, following the expense of building and maintaining the New Palace in Darmstadt, they were far from rich.

A happy childhood

Alix was brought up to follow the old-fashioned English virtue of 'waste not, want not'. The children's clothes and toys were simple and the food was plain. Not that the little Princess Alix cared very much for dolls. To her, they did not seem 'real' enough. Her naturally warm and loving nature drew her instead to animals – dogs and cats that responded to the child's careful caresses.

Children's party games were all great favourites with her. But the greatest favourite of all was dressing up. All the old boxes in her mother's wardrobe would be raided and brought out, and Alix and her brother and sisters would teeter around in the long, twisting corridors of the New Palace in high heels, boots, crinolines and furs, pretending, as they descended the grand staircase, to be fairy kings and queens.

Despite Nanny Orchard's strict regime, the children were full of impish fun. A small pony carriage with a liveried footman at its head, designed to carry the children about the palace grounds, was often seen to career about wildly. One day, while playing a mad game of hide and seek with her brother Ernie, the six-year-old Alix fell through some glass panes in the garden. Her legs were badly cut by the glass, and she was to carry the scars of her adventurous high spirits all her life.

Summers were often spent in one of the fairytale castles overlooking the Rhine. But winters were always spent in Darmstadt. Christmas in the New Palace was a particularly memorable occasion – a great family feast in which the

_{Hulton-Deutsch Collection}

_{Hulton-Deutsch Collection}

♛ *The Palace at Gatchina* left, *the place of Nicholas's upbringing, had more than 900 rooms, yet the future Tsar's bedroom was spartan – he slept on an army bunk with hard pillows. Life was rigorous, and education, by a succession of tutors, was strict. Nicholas's most important tutor was the intensely unpopular Constantin Petrovich Pobedonostsev – a leader of the Russian Orthodox Church – whose influence on the young Tsarevich's life can be seen from the grotesque contemporary caricature* above

_{John Massey Stewart}

Mansell Collection

♕ *The family home at the New Palace, Darmstadt* above *held many cherished memories for Alix. Until the death of her brother Frederick, life was blissfully happy here. Most of all, however, Alix delighted in her yearly visits to England to stay with her beloved grandmother* left, *the ageing Queen Victoria. Although the old Queen adored all her grandchildren, 'Alicky' was one of her firmest favourites. 'Alicky' in turn referred to Victoria as 'Grandmama in England'*

Archiv für Kunst und Geschichte, Berlin

THE DEATH OF ALEXANDER II

On 13 March 1881, Nicholas's grandfather Alexander II was assassinated as he drove through the streets of St Petersburg. A bomb was thrown, shattering the carriage but, ironically, leaving the Tsar unhurt. As he stepped from the carriage, however, a second bomb was thrown which mutilated him, tearing off his legs. Alexander was brought to the Winter Palace to die – a scene which Nicholas, then aged 13, would never forget

entire household took part. But the poor of the town were not forgotten. Princess Alice made sure that gifts from her family were sent to all the hospitals – a tradition that Alix was later to continue as Tsarina.

Perhaps the most delightful of Alix's childhood memories were the visits to England to stay with her beloved grandmother, Queen Victoria. Alexandra would later delight in recalling to her own envious children the walks around the grounds of Balmoral and joyful memories of paddling and crab-hunting in English seaside resorts.

Tragedy strikes

Then, one day in November 1878, tragedy struck Darmstadt when the incurable disease of diphtheria broke out in the New Palace. The entire family, with the exception of Princess Ella, went down with it. For a while, Princess Alix was the most dangerously ill of all of them. On 12 November, her mother telegraphed Queen Victoria. 'This is dreadful,' she wrote, 'my sweet precious Alicky so ill. The doctor at once saw that it was a severe case.'

At that time, in the absence of vaccination and other forms of preventive treatment, there was simply nothing that the medical profession could do. Grand Duchess Alice nursed her daughter constantly, sitting up with her the whole night, and going anxiously from one bed to another of her stricken family.

On 16 November, the youngest daughter, May, died. The other children, including Alix, began to pull through. But the Grand Duchess herself was exhausted. On 8 December, she too fell ill. She could no longer hold on, and finally passed away on 14 December 1878, aged 35, amid scenes of terrible family grief. Alix, only six years old, was devastated.

After her mother's death, Princess Alix spent much of her childhood in England where Queen Victoria personally supervised her upbringing and took it upon herself to ensure that she received a first-class English

education. Alix was an excellent student who enjoyed most subjects, particularly politics, and had developed into a fine pianist. Her favourite tutor was an Englishwoman, Margaret Jackson, known as 'Madgie'.

The first meeting

In Russia, Nicholas was educated by a succession of tutors. But the most important one, Constantin Pobedonostsev, was a bigot, full of radical and religious prejudices, who opposed all reforms and, above all, hated parliaments and free elections. But he was also a brilliant teacher, and his job was to instil in Nicholas's impressionable young mind the importance of his mission as the future Tsar of Russia.

Pobedonostsev taught Nicholas that the Tsars were appointed by a God whose will must never be challenged, and that any

opposition from the people must, therefore, be crushed. In March 1881, something happened which seemed to Nicholas to underline the truth of his tutor's teachings. Nicholas's grandfather, Tsar Alexander II, known as the Tsar-Liberator because he freed the serfs, was blown to pieces by a terrorist bomb. The dying Tsar was brought to the Winter Palace in St Petersburg, and Nicholas, aged 13, watched in horror from the end of the bed as the doctors announced, 'The Emperor is dead.'

From that day, Nicholas's father, Alexander III, vowed that he would rule Russia with an iron hand – all opposition was to be ruthlessly crushed. He was determined that his son would one day uphold the absolute authority of the Tsar.

Nicholas accepted the views of his father and his tutor Pobedonostsev. But, unlike his

By gracious permission of HM the Queen

Tsar Alexander II m. Marie of Hesse
(1818-1881) (1824-1880)

Tsar Alexander III m. Marie Fedorovna
(1845-1894) (Princess Dagmar)
(1847-1918)

Alexis
(1850-1908)

Grand Duke Paul m. Alexandra
(1860-1919) (1870-1891)

Grand Duke m. Grand Duchess
Vladimir Marie Pavlovna
(1847-1909) (1854-1920)

Grand Duke Serge m. Elizabeth of Hesse
(1857-1905) (Ella)
(1864-1918)

Grand Duke Cyril Grand Duke Boris Grand Duke Andrei
(1876-1938) (1877-1943) (1879-1956)

Grand Duke Dimitry
(1891-1942)

Grand Duke George Grand Duchess Xenia m. Grand Duke
(1871-1899) (1875-1960) Alexander Mikhailovich
(Sandro) (1866-1933)

Grand Duke Michael Grand Duchess Olga
(1878-1918) (1882-1960)

Tsar Nicholas II
(1868-1918)

Irina m. Prince Felix
Yussoupov

Grand Duchess Olga
(1895-1918)

Grand Duchess Marie
(1899-1918)

Grand Duchess Tatiana
(1897-1918)

Grand Duchess Anastasia
(1901-1918)

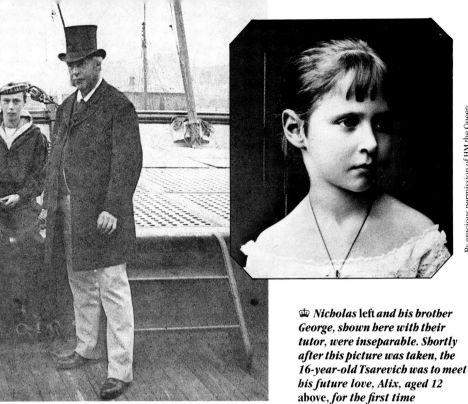

By gracious permission of HM the Queen

♛ **Nicholas** left **and his brother George, shown here with their tutor, were inseparable. Shortly after this picture was taken, the 16-year-old Tsarevich was to meet his future love, Alix, aged 12** above, **for the first time**

father, he did not look or act like a great autocrat. Instead, he was an extremely charming young man, quite short and thin, with a smile described by a friend as 'tender, shy, slightly sad'.

In 1884, Princess Alix, aged 12, arrived in St Petersburg for the first time to attend the wedding of her sister, Ella, to Grand Duke Serge, Nicholas's uncle. The wedding was held in the Winter Palace and Alix watched in awe as a golden coach drawn by white horses carried her sister to the chapel. During the wedding service, she caught the eye of the 16-year-old Nicholas. He would never forget what she was wearing that day – a white muslin dress with roses in her hair. A few days later, at a children's party, he pressed a small brooch into her hand. Flattered, she accepted at first, but then shyly returned the gift.

The Hesse-Romanov Alliance

Queen Victoria m. Prince Albert of Saxe-Coburg
(1819-1901) (1819-1861)

Princess Victoria m. Frederick III German Emperor (1840-1901) (1831-1888)

Albert m. King Edward VII of England (1841-1910)

Princess Alexandra of Denmark (1844-1925)

Prince Leopold (1853-1884)

Princess Beatrice (1857-1944)

Kaiser William II (1859-1941)

Princess Alice m. Louis IV Grand Duke of Hesse (1843-1878) (1837-1892)

Princess Victoria m. Louis of Hesse of Battenberg (1863-1950) (1854-1921)

Princess Irene of Hesse (1866-1953)

Ernest (1868-1937)

Frederick (1870-1873)

Princess Mary of Hesse (May) (1874-1878)

Princess Elizabeth of Hesse (Ella) m. Grand Duke Serge (1864-1918)

Princess Alix of Hesse (1872-1918)

Tsarevich Alexis (1904-1918)

Alice m. Prince Andrew of Greece (1885-1969) (1882-1944)

Louis Earl Mountbatten of Burma (1900-1979)

Prince Philip Duke of Edinburgh (1921-)

7

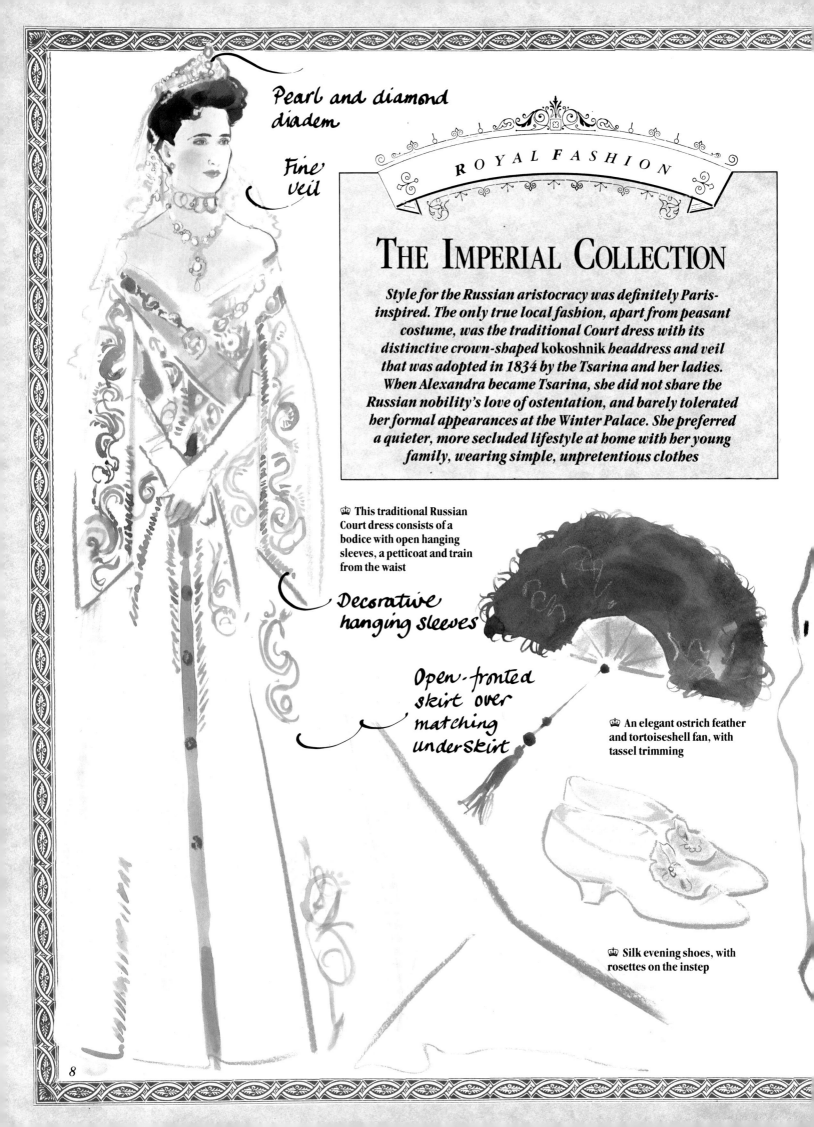

Pearl and diamond diadem

Fine veil

THE IMPERIAL COLLECTION

Style for the Russian aristocracy was definitely Paris-inspired. The only true local fashion, apart from peasant costume, was the traditional Court dress with its distinctive crown-shaped kokoshnik headdress and veil that was adopted in 1834 by the Tsarina and her ladies. When Alexandra became Tsarina, she did not share the Russian nobility's love of ostentation, and barely tolerated her formal appearances at the Winter Palace. She preferred a quieter, more secluded lifestyle at home with her young family, wearing simple, unpretentious clothes

♛ This traditional Russian Court dress consists of a bodice with open hanging sleeves, a petticoat and train from the waist

Decorative hanging sleeves

Open-fronted skirt over matching underskirt

♛ An elegant ostrich feather and tortoiseshell fan, with tassel trimming

♛ Silk evening shoes, with rosettes on the instep

Nuptial
Crown

False
ringlets

Lee Boltin/Photri

♛ The Nuptial Crown,
worn by all the brides
in the Russian
Imperial Family, was
made from pieces of
the diamond belt of
Catherine the Great

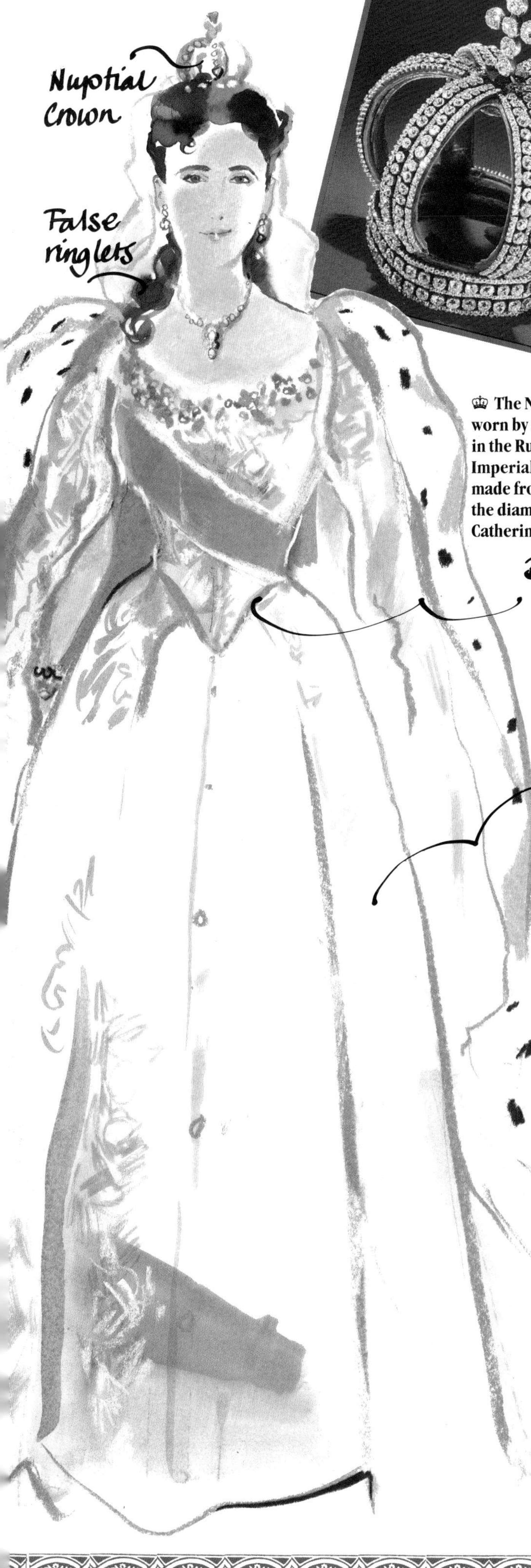

Bodice
forming
a deep
'V' shape

Overskirt
completely
covered in silver
thread embroidery

♛ The wedding dress of
silver tissue was heavily
embroidered down the open
front, on the hanging sleeves
and the train

♛ The bridegroom
wore the pale blue
riband of St Andrew
over his Russian
Hussar's uniform

Deep Bertha collar with rows of ribbon insertion

Feathers dyed to match artificial flowers

♛ Two summer hats in straw, trimmed with flowers and dyed feathers

Wide sleeves with matching ribbon insertion

♛ Sofia's jewelled bouquet holder is made of gold, with small diamonds and sapphires

Novosti Press Agency

Two deep flounces of lace at the hem

♛ The most seductive fashion of the period, the tea-gown was designed for entertaining at home. In fine silk, lavishly embroidered and ruffled, Alexandra wore these gowns in her mauve boudoir

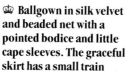 Ballgown in silk velvet and beaded net with a pointed bodice and little cape sleeves. The graceful skirt has a small train

Deep swags of diamanté and pearl embroidery on net

Small fantail train with matching embroidery

Hulton-Deutsch Collection

♔ Both Nicholas and Alexandra preferred a simple tailored style to the conventional over-elaborate Court dress

♔ Exquisite long kid gloves were for evening wear

Mansell Collection

STAR-CROSSED LOVERS

THE OBSCURE GERMAN PRINCESS WAS NOT CONSIDERED A WORTHY MATCH FOR NICHOLAS. BUT, SURE IN HIS LOVE FOR ALEXANDRA, HE OVERCAME OPPOSITION AND PROPOSED

By gracious permission of HM the Queen

♔ *Nicholas enthusiastically courted the young Alix during her visit to St Petersburg in 1889. The 17-year-old Princess may have lacked the sophistication to impress Russian society but her natural charms were enough to enrapture the Tsarevich*

A S THE HEIR TO THE THRONE, THE TSAREVICH Nicholas lived very much under the shadow of his father. Alexander III was a powerful Tsar. He ruthlessly crushed all who opposed him, but he also helped modernize Russia. Under his rule, new roads, railways, and factories were built. As a child, Nicholas could feel only awe at all his father's achievements.

At 21, Nicholas was popular and likeable, if slightly shy and timid. He spoke fluent German and French, as well as English with a perfect upper-class accent. He was a fine horseman, a superb dancer and an excellent shot.

After their first meeting, Nicholas did not forget the beautiful Princess Alix, nor she him. But in 1889, aged 17, she received a marriage proposal from Prince Albert Victor, known as Prince Eddy, the eldest son of the Prince of Wales.

Queen Victoria wrote to a friend: 'I hear all hope of Alicky's marrying Eddy is at an end. She has written to tell him how it pains her to pain him, but that she cannot marry him, much as she likes him as a cousin, that she knows she would not be happy with him and that he would not be happy with her.'

The next meeting

In the spring of 1889, when Alix visited Russia again to stay with her sister Ella in St Petersburg, Nicholas became a frequent visitor to the house. The attraction between the couple was stronger than ever.

Alix was tall, with long golden tresses and stunning blue-grey eyes. Outwardly, she was serious and somewhat shy, but Nicholas sensed that great passions lay beneath her cool exterior.

He took her out ice skating, and in the evenings escorted her to balls and concerts and even managed to persuade his parents to organize a tea-dance for her.

Socially, however, Alix's visit was not a success. Her clothes appeared plain compared to the rich society women. Unfortunately for Nicholas, his parents opposed any closer liaison between the couple. The Tsar wanted to marry his son and heir to a French noblewoman in order to strengthen Russia's alliance with France. Alix was minor German Royalty and, because she was an extremely devout Protestant, it was assumed that she would never agree to convert to the Russian Orthodox Church – as would inevitably be required of her.

And so they parted. Alix had fallen in love with Nicholas but she hid it carefully at first. It was only on her return to Darmstadt that she realized she had left her heart in Russia.

Nicholas, still in Russia, had little else to do at the age of 22 but enjoy the life of a playboy.

Mansell Collection

He forsook his official duties in favour of an endless round of balls, receptions and private parties. He had also received an excellent military education from his tutor, General Danilov, and his tastes and interests were typical of the average young Russian Guards officer of his day. Nicholas had been given command of a squadron of horse guards by his father, and he often went with them to their barracks in Krasnoe Selo outside St Petersburg.

It was about this time, in 1890, that Nicholas began to receive the ardent attentions of a brilliant young ballerina from the Imperial Ballet, Mathilde Kschessinska. Mathilde was convinced that the heir to the throne was in love with her, as she undoubtedly was with him.

Enduring love

Nicholas, although attentive to Mathilde, had still not forgotten Alix. On hearing that she had returned to Russia to visit her sister at her country estate, Nicholas wrote, with great emotion, in his diary, 'Oh Lord, how I want to go to visit her there! If I do not see her now, I shall have to wait a whole year and that will be hard.'

In a state of almost unbearable longing to see his love again, Nicholas departed, in October 1890, on a long and arduous Royal tour.

Accompanied by his brother George, his cousin, Prince George of Greece, and several Russian noblemen, he went to Athens and then to Egypt. He journeyed eastward to Hong Kong, Saigon, Singapore and Bangkok, where he was received by the King of Siam. During his visit to Japan, he was almost murdered when he was attacked by a Japanese swordsman.

On his return to St Petersburg, Nicholas became involved again with the ballerina, Kschessinska.

But still he could not forget his blonde Princess; in the summer of 1892, he wrote in his diary: 'My dream is one day to marry Alix H. I have loved her for a long time, and still deeper and stronger since 1889, when she spent six weeks in St Petersburg. For a long time, I resisted my feeling that my dream will come true.'

At last, in the spring of 1894, his chance came. The most prominent members of the European aristocracy were due to gather in Germany for the wedding in Coburg of Alix's brother, Ernest. Nicholas went straight to his father, declared his love for Alix and begged him to relent and allow him finally to propose

> ## 'My dream is one day to marry Alix H...'
>
> NICHOLAS'S DIARY, 1892

Hulton-Deutsch Collection

👑 *The marriage proposal of Prince Eddy (the eldest son of the Prince of Wales) above was turned down by Alix in 1889. Queen Victoria commented on her strength of character as the Princess stood firm against the wishes of both families – she had already decided against a marriage of convenience*

Mansell Collection

THE GRAND TOUR

Nicholas was away for two years (1890-2), visiting countries as far afield as Egypt, India – where he was equally irritated by the heat and the British – Hong Kong and Japan. In Japan, an attempt was made on his life by a swordsman who suddenly, and for no apparent reason, lunged at him, gashing him severely on the forehead. The assailant was overpowered by his companions, but Nicholas was to bear the scar of the attack and deep prejudice against Japan – referring to the people of Japan as 'monkeys' – for the rest of his life marriage to her when they were in Coburg.

The Tsar was reluctant. This was not what he had hoped for and planned for his son. Now, for the first time in his life, Nicholas stood up to his father and said that if he could not marry Alix, then he would never marry. Alarmed at this prospect, the Tsar eventually relented.

In April 1894, Nicholas, accompanied by three of his uncles, boarded a train from St Petersburg for Coburg. Alix was waiting at the station, and that evening, as they dined together, they could scarcely contain their excitement at being together once more.

The long-awaited proposal

The following morning, Nicholas went to Alix's rooms and proposed. Later, he wrote in his diary: 'She looked particularly pretty, but extremely sad. They left us alone and then began between us the talk that I had long ago so strongly wanted and, at the same time, very much feared. We talked till twelve, but with no result; she still objects to changing her religion. Poor girl, she cried a lot. But she was calmer when we parted.'

It was a crisis for Alix. Torn between her love and her religion, she cried a great deal that day, whispering again and again the chilling words 'No, I cannot.' Fortunately for Nicholas, help was at hand. Queen Victoria, who was in Coburg for the wedding, did her best to persuade Alix to accept Nicholas and agree to convert to Russian Orthodoxy. Alix's family also advised her to consent. On the day after the wedding, Alix's resistance crumbled.

A day of joy

'Today is the first day of my engagement to my darling, adorable Alix,' wrote Nicholas. 'A marvellous, unforgettable day. Oh God, what a mountain has rolled from my shoulders. The whole day I have been walking in a dream, without fully realizing what has been happening to me.'

After breakfast, the radiant couple went to have coffee with Queen Victoria, who was delighted with the engagement and revelled in the company of the young lovers.

Ten days of bliss followed, during which the couple walked, talked and dined together.

Recalling the opposition to the match, Alix wrote a moving letter to the Empress who replied to Nicholas: 'Alix is quite like a daughter to me now.' As a token of her new-found love and respect, the Empress sent Alix a superb Easter egg inlaid with precious gems and designed by the great Russian jeweller, Fabergé.

Soon, the time approached when the couple had to part. Alone, they were tender and relaxed with each other. To Nicholas, who had waited so long, it felt unnatural for them to be

Mansell Collection

apart even for one night. He spent the last evening with her alone. 'How good we were together. A paradise,' he wrote. Both Nicholas and Alix had realized how much happier they were in each other's company than with strangers, with whom they both felt uneasy.

Sadly for the happy couple, Nicholas soon had to return to his family in Russia. 'Only now, I am wearing a ring on my finger. It makes me feel strange,' he said.

A month later, the couple reunited in England and travelled to Walton-on-Thames to stay with Alix's eldest sister. At Windsor, they stayed with a delighted Victoria. Here, Nicholas presented his engagement gifts to Alix, which included a priceless sapphire and diamond brooch and a *sautoir* of pearls also created by Fabergé, a gift from the Tsar.

While in England, the couple became godparents to 'David', the future Edward VIII, a king destined to lose his throne. Before leaving England, Alix wrote in her fiancé's diary: 'I am yours, you are mine, of that be sure. You are locked in my heart, the little key is lost and now you must stay there forever.'

The new Tsar

But their joy was suddenly and cruelly interrupted. Nicholas had returned to Russia to find Tsar Alexander III seriously ill. Alix was summoned at once. For ten tormented days, they kept a vigil at his bedside. But it was to no avail. In the presence of the whole Imperial Family, Father John of Kronstadt performed the last rites. Alexander died on 1 November 1894 and Nicholas II became the new Tsar.

The next morning, in the presence of

👑 *Left alone in St Petersburg, Nicholas responded to the attentions paid to him by the brilliant young ballerina Mathilde Kschessinska. He gave her gifts and even set her up in a small house of her own. His father, the Tsar, appeared to approve of the affair*

Nicholas and the Empress Marie, Alix was received into the Russian Orthodox Church. 'Even in our great grief, God gives us a sweet and luminous joy,' wrote Nicholas. 'At ten o'clock in the presence only of the family, my dear Alix has been consecrated to Orthodoxy.' After the service, Alix, Marie and Nicholas took Holy Communion together. When they returned to the Palace, the Tsar issued his first Imperial Decree, proclaiming Alix's new faith and title. She was now 'the truly believing Grand Duchess Alexandra Fedorovna'.

Nicholas was left with awesome responsibilities, for which, at 26, he was ill-prepared. He clung to Alix, and they both decided to get married as soon as possible. And thus, Alexandra's first Royal entry into St Petersburg was in a solemn funeral procession.

Mary Evans Picture Library

DEATH OF A TSAR

On 1 November 1894, Tsar Alexander III died at his summer palace at Livadia. Ten days earlier, Alix had been summoned and, in his bedroom, seated in his armchair, the dying Tsar gave the young couple his Royal blessing – at last, Alix and Nicholas were formally betrothed. But rather than a wedding, Alix's first Royal duty was to be a ride through St Petersburg as part of a funeral cortège

Hulton-Deutsch Collection

Archiv für Kunst und Geschichte, Berlin

By gracious permission of HM the Queen

👑 *Queen Victoria – pictured with Alix, Nicholas and other guests at the wedding in Coburg of Alix's brother* far left *– championed Nicholas's cause when Alix had doubts about converting to the Russian Orthodox religion. The day after the wedding, Alix accepted Nicholas* left, *and for ten days they enjoyed celebrations. 'It seems that the whole of Russia has sent flowers to my bride,' Nicholas wrote in his diary*

15

A Dream Come True

A week after the Tsar's funeral, on 26 November 1894, Nicholas and Alexandra were married. Many of the guests who had come for the funeral stayed on to celebrate the wedding.

On the morning of the wedding, the Dowager Empress Marie took her future daughter-in-law to the Winter Palace where the ceremony was to take place.

As troops and crowds lined the streets outside, Nicholas, wearing a Hussar's uniform, arrived at the Winter Palace. The ceremony was straightforward and simple and, out of respect for the late Tsar, no festivities were allowed. 'One day in deepest mourning, lamenting a loved one, the next, in smartest clothes being married,' was how Alexandra described it.

Immediately after the ceremony, the young couple drove to the Anitchkov Palace, enthusiastically cheered by huge crowds. As the marriage had been arranged so hastily, no proper preparations had been made for the couple and they agreed to stay as the guests of Nicholas's mother. The rooms they shared at the Anitchkov Palace with Marie were cramped and lacking in privacy.

In these small rooms, Alexandra sat all day, moving into her bedroom when her husband had to receive official visitors in the sitting room. But she was entirely happy; her husband was always near her.

Continuing the line

In December 1894, the couple went to the Alexander Palace at Tsarskoye Selo, the fabled 'Village of the Tsars', where they would settle. Being under the same roof as her mother-in-law, seeing her every day and competing with her for her husband's attentions had not been easy for Alexandra. In Tsarskoye Selo, true happiness blossomed.

Nicholas wrote in his diary: 'Every hour that passes, I bless the Lord from the bottom of my soul for the happiness which he has granted me. My love and admiration for Alix continually grow. There are no words capable of describing the bliss it is to be living together.'

Below this entry, Alexandra wrote, 'Ever more and more, stronger and deeper, grow my love and devotion, and my longing for you. Never can I thank God enough for the treasure he has given me for my very own — and to be called yours, darling, what happiness can be greater? God bless you my beloved little husband. I cover your sweet face with kisses.'

In the spring of 1895, Alexandra learned that she was expecting a baby.

Mansell Collection

Mansell Collection

AN IMPERIAL CELEBRATION

On the morning of 26 November 1894, Alexandra was escorted from her sister's palace by the Dowager Empress Marie to the Winter Palace where the wedding ceremony was to take place.

In the Malachite Drawing Room, Alexandra was formally dressed in front of the famous gold mirror of former empresses. Assisted by the chief dressers of the ladies of the Imperial Family, her hair was done in traditional long side curls. The crown jewels, which lay on red velvet cushions, were handed to her and Marie herself placed the diamond nuptial crown on her daughter-in-law's head.

Decked in numerous splendid diamond ornaments, Alexandra shimmered from head to toe. Her dress was of real silver tissue, and from her shoulders flowed the Imperial mantle of cloth of gold, lined with fur.

The Palace guards lined the stairs as the wedding guests started to arrive *left*. Nicholas, wearing a Hussar's uniform, joined his bride in the Malachite Drawing Room *top left* before the ceremony and they welcomed family and friends of royal ranking. Included among the guests were many dignitaries such as the Prince and Princess of Wales and George, the Duke of York, who had come for the funeral of the old Tsar and stayed for the wedding of the new.

Marie and Alexandra then walked through the Winter Palace galleries *centre left* to the chapel where Nicholas was waiting. Conducted by the Metropolitan of the Orthodox Church, the religion that had almost been a stumbling block to the love match, the ceremony took place and they became man and wife *bottom left*.

'She looked too wonderfully lovely,' said the Princess of Wales. The Duke of York wrote: 'I never saw two people more in love with each other'

ILN Picture Library

Mary Evans Picture Library

Robert Hunt Library

Robert Hunt Library

THE WEDDING OF NICHOLAS II
CZAR OF RUSSIA
· NOVEMBER · 26 · 1894 ·

17

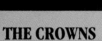

Novosti Press Agency

THE ORB

Catherine the Great's symbolic orb was made of solid gold, banded with diamonds, and was topped by a huge 47-carat sapphire

Novosti Press Agency

THE CROWNS

The Tsar's Grand Imperial Crown *below* was originally made for the Coronation of Catherine the Great. It is studded with 5012 diamonds, totalling about 3000 carats. 76 oriental pearls curve over the crown which is topped by a huge ruby spinel, bought for 'a load of gold ingots' from a Manchu emperor in 1676. The smaller crown *above* was worn by the Tsarina

Novosti Press Agency

THE SCEPTRE

A truly splendid example, the sceptre was topped by an enormous 193-carat diamond. It was given to Catherine by one of her lovers, Prince Gregory Orlov

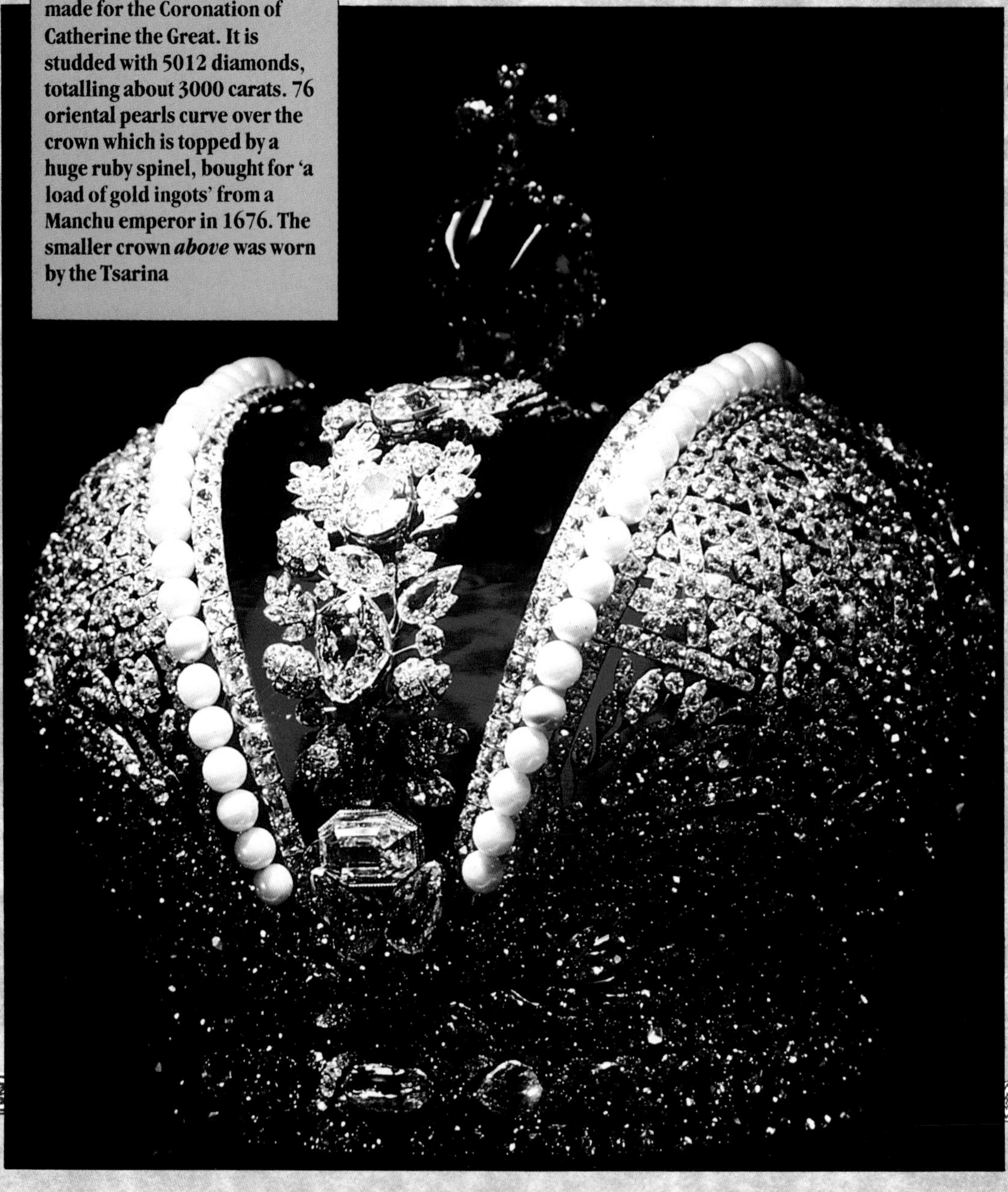

THE ROMANOV LEGACY

Much of the magnificent Russian Imperial Regalia was made for the Coronation of Catherine the Great in 1762. Although, after the 1917 Revolution, the Soviets disposed of many items, those that remain are now on display in the Armoury of the Kremlin in Moscow as a reminder of a very different past

Edimedia

♛ The royal jeweller, Peter Carl Fabergé, made the enamelled coat of arms *above* for Nicholas II

♛ The fabulous 'pink' diamond is the centrepiece of the Imperial Diadem *right*. It was made in 1810

Novosti Press Agency

♛ One of the greatest of Russia's national heroes, Alexander Nevsky, defeated the Teutonic Knights in 1242. The Order *above* is named after him

♛ The superb gold and silver clasp *right*, studded with Indian and Brazilian diamonds, was made in 1750 for the Coronation mantle worn by the Empress Elizabeth

Novosti Press Agency

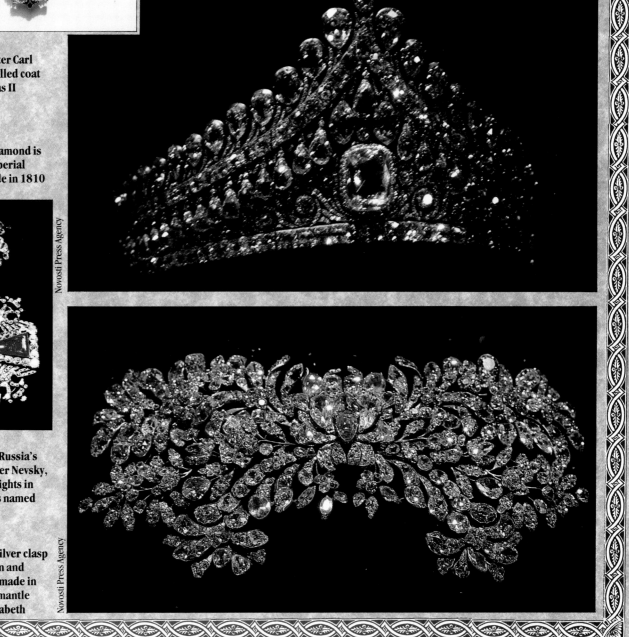

Novosti Press Agency

CROWNED IN GLORY

ALEXANDRA'S WHOLE LIFE REVOLVED AROUND HER FAMILY. YET PRIVATE HAPPINESS HAD TO BE TEMPERED BY THE DUTIES OF STATE. ON CORONATION DAY, THE POMP AND SPLENDOUR ALSO BROUGHT TERRIBLE TRAGEDY

Jean-Loup Charmet

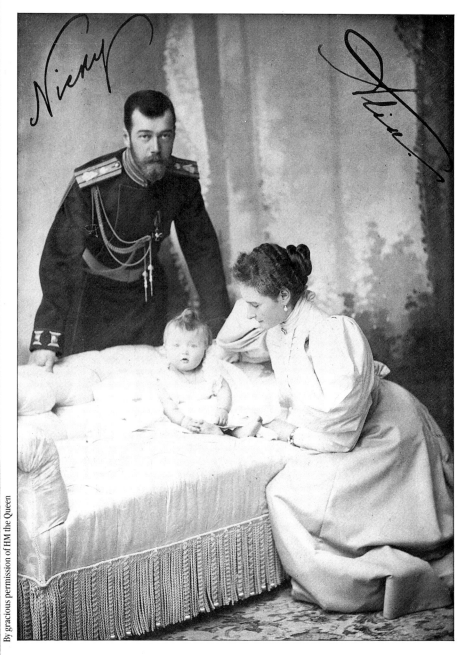

By gracious permission of HM the Queen

👑 *Nicholas and Alexandra with their first-born, the Grand Duchess Olga, in 1896*

O N 15 NOVEMBER 1895, THE GRAND DUCHESS Olga was born. As the guns of the Fortress of Peter and Paul thundered out the announcement of the birth, the people of St Petersburg eagerly counted the shots. Three hundred would mean a son, a hundred and one, a daughter.

At the christening, the baby was taken to the church at Tsarskoye Selo in a gold coach, like a fairy princess, a mantle of gold covering her little body. 'You can imagine our intense happiness now that we have such a precious little being of our own to care for and look after,' wrote Alexandra to her sister.

Alexandra had often been lonely during her first year in Russia, as Nicholas's responsibilities kept him very busy. Now, she devoted herself to the baby, and knitted endless jackets and socks for her. But ahead of her, in the spring, lay another event, quite different from the gentle domesticity of tending a first-born: the Coronation of the new Tsar and Tsarina.

Preparing for power

In the days before the Coronation, Nicholas and Alexandra went into retreat at the Petrovsky Palace outside Moscow to prepare themselves for the ceremony with prayers and fasting. In the meantime, representatives of nearly all the royal houses of Europe arrived in the capital.

According to tradition, the uncrowned Tsar could not enter Moscow until the day before his Coronation. On the sunny afternoon of 25 May 1896, the Tsar and his entourage made their formal entry into the city. The state entrance to the Kremlin was decorated sumptuously. Huge crowds lined the streets, from well-dressed ladies to peasants in their Sunday best, crossing themselves in emotion as the procession passed. At the head of the procession rode Nicholas, surrounded by all the Grand Dukes and foreign Princes. The Empresses followed in the beautiful gilt state coaches, their panels painted by the noted French 18th-century court painter, François Boucher.

The Dowager Empress, Marie, went first. As she had already been crowned, 13 years previously, her coach was surmounted by a crown. The Empress Alexandra Fedorovna drove alone, as yet no crown on her coach. The long procession through the city lasted several hours. When it reached the Iverskaia gates, all disembarked and the Empress entered the chapel of Our Lady, which contained the celebrated 'Iverskaia', a greatly venerated icon.

The Coronation ceremony

The Coronation itself took place the next day, 26 May, in the old Ouspensky Cathedral — a magnificent setting for so impressive a ceremony.

The Cathedral had suffered greatly at the hands of Napoleon and his invading armies in 1812 but, since then, had been greatly restored. Now, it was unveiled in its ancient splendour. All the walls and pillars were covered with 15th-century frescoes depicting the Saints and scenes from the Bible.

The uniforms and robes worn by the Imperial party were woven from the finest fabrics. Fabulous jewels were on display. The Grand Duchess Ella, Alix's sister, wore her famous emeralds and the old Grand Duchess Constantine wore her fabulous sapphires, every flawless stone two inches across. And as a backdrop to these sparkling bosoms, the altar screen of the Cathedral glittered with the purest gold and

Hulton-Deutsch Collection

Hulton-Deutsch Collection

👑 Left *By tradition, the coronation ceremony of a Russian Tsar was always held in Moscow, which was deemed worthier for such an occasion than the rather more artificial and westernized capital of St Petersburg. The photograph of Nicholas's entry into Moscow the day before his Coronation shows part of the procession of coaches following the Tsar into the Kremlin. The State Coach in front, carrying Alexandra, as yet bears no crown, in recognition of the future Tsarina's uncrowned state. The morning after the procession, heralds in historic costume* above *proclaimed that on this day, 26 May 1896, a Tsar would be crowned*

silver, encircling icons of priceless beauty.

As the Coronation ceremony would last five hours, it began early. The Emperor and Empress walked to the Cathedral in a State Procession from the Kremlin. First came the Dowager Empress Marie, pale and serious, as if recalling her own happy Coronation 13 years earlier. After her, each walking under a separate canopy, came Nicholas and Alexandra, attended by numerous courtiers in splendid uniforms. The Dowager Empress blazed with diamonds. The young Empress had no jewels, except for a string of pearls around her neck. At first flushed and nervous, she steadily grew in composure.

A splendid ceremony

The Emperor wore the uniform of Russia's oldest regiment, the Preobrajensky. Nicholas had wanted to wear the robes of the ancient Tsars and their old, lighter crown, but iron etiquette insisted that he must wear the Imperial Crown, weighing nine pounds. This caused considerable pain as his forehead was still sensitive from the scar inflicted by the Japanese fanatic during his Far Eastern tour.

Before the altar stood members of the Russian Orthodox high clergy: metropolitans, archbishops, bishops and abbots – while at the front of the Cathedral, two coronation chairs awaited the future Tsar and Tsarina. Nicholas sat on the 17th-century Diamond Throne of Tsar Alexis – so named for the 870 diamonds encrusted in its surface. Alexandra sat next to her husband on the Ivory Throne – brought to Russia from Byzantium in the 15th century.

To Alexandra, the Coronation was a time of intense emotion. Her head whirled with its mystic splendour and beauty and she felt as though she was becoming one with Russia, sealed for ever in its heart and soul. As she knelt in deep prayer with the entire congregation, the Metropolitan of the Russian Orthodox Church led a prayer for the Tsar. How Alexandra's heart went out to Nicholas when he knelt, this time all alone, while the others stood and prayed for Russia and his people. Next, the couple received Holy Communion and the Metropolitan anointed the Tsar with holy oils. Nicholas then entered the Sanctuary and received the Blessed Sacrament, just like a priest.

A bad omen

As Nicholas approached the altar steps, the chain of the Order of St Andrew fell to the ground. This would have been a bad omen to the superstitious, so orders were quickly given to hush up the incident. But Alexandra was not troubled by this. She witnessed only the sunbeam that fell at that moment on her husband's head, which seemed to her a halo, so transported was she by the rituals.

Giraudon/Musée d'Orsay

Mary Evans Picture Library

A GLITTERING OCCASION

The five-hour Coronation began with a mass, followed by the formal robing of the couple. Then came the anointing with the holy oil *left*, the swearing of the Tsar's oath, and the Coronation itself, in which Nicholas, according to tradition, took the huge Imperial Crown from the robed Metropolitan *above* and placed it on his own head for a moment. *Far right* The final stage. Nicholas touched Alexandra's head with the crown before replacing it on his head – this time for the duration of the ceremony.
The official declaration was prepared *right* and then the souvenir machine went into action. Also shown *right* is a celebratory coronation cup

Mary Evans Picture Library

The procession left the Cathedral on foot and returned to the Kremlin with the Royal couple at the head. Bells pealed in all the 'forty times forty' Moscow churches, cannon thundered and crowds roared.

A great banquet for 7000 guests was held in the Council Chamber of the former Tsars. According to tradition Nicholas and Alexandra dined alone, seated under a canopy wearing their robes and crowns. Foreign ambassadors drank to the Emperor's health while foreign royalty looked down from the upper gallery of the great hall, for only Russians could take part in the banquet itself. During the meal, foreign ambassadors were admitted one by one to drink the health of the Imperial couple.

Nicholas and Alexandra spent the rest of the day greeting their other guests – he still wearing the huge Imperial Crown and she still in her magnificent dress.

A city celebrates

As evening fell at the Kremlin, Alexandra had pressed a button hidden in a bouquet of roses. Moscow was immediately set ablaze with thousands of lights – a glimmering fairy city.

Throughout the celebrations, Alexandra looked radiant, as if reflecting the wonders that surrounded her. Her sister, Ella, looked especially magnificent in a Court gown of cream velvet embroidered with golden fuchsias. Other Grand Duchesses wore dresses of cloth-of-gold embroidered with autumn leaves, irises and other flowers. The immense, bearded Emir of Bokhara, in oriental robes and wearing a Russian general's epaulettes made out of diamonds, caught the attention of the crowds, as did the Emperor of China's envoy, Li-Hung-Chang, unforgettable in yellow mandarin robes and peacock feathers.

Several balls and gala performances of opera and ballet had been planned to follow the Coronation. But disaster was to follow.

A shocking outcome

According to tradition, the day after the Coronation belonged to the Muscovites, and a huge open-air feast for the people – to be attended by Nicholas and Alexandra – was arranged. The authorities had ordered hundreds of barrels of free beer that were to be distributed among the people, along with enamelled souvenir cups.

Although many people were expected, it soon became clear that the authorities had vastly miscalculated numbers. A huge crowd gathered, eagerly awaiting their gifts. At first, all was well but, as the cartloads of beer began to arrive, a rumour started that there was not enough beer to go round, and that only those who got there first would receive any. Within

23

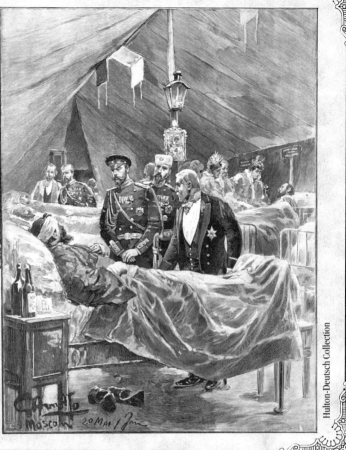

TRAGEDY AT KHODYNKA

The day after the Tsar's Coronation, a huge crowd of peasants gathered at Khodynka – a field outside Moscow – for an open-air feast arranged by the authorities. But as carts bearing their promised bundles of free gifts arrived, a wild stampede set in and thousands were trampled to death. Devastated, Nicholas and Alexandra spent days visiting the injured in hospital. Despite their efforts, the incident did little to enhance their popularity, and many people saw the disaster as an omen of doom for the new Tsar's reign

minutes, what had started as a good-natured outing suddenly became an ugly scene, as people started to run and push each other in their hurry to reach the carts. The small group of Cossacks that was on hand to keep order was soon brushed aside, and people tripped and stumbled into the ditches and trenches – soon to be trampled underfoot by the crowds. By the time the police had arrived, Khodynka looked like a battlefield.

At first, the full extent of the horror was kept from Nicholas. When he finally found out what had happened, he was horrified. Both he and Alexandra immediately wanted to cancel the Grand Ball scheduled to take place at the French Embassy that evening. But his advisers implored him to attend so as not to offend their French hosts – Russia's major ally. Nicholas and

Alexandra relented and attended, their faces red with tears. Alexandra went through the motions like an automaton.

When the Imperial couple visited the hospitals, full of casualties, they were both deeply moved. The Tsar immediately ordered that the dead be buried in individual coffins at his own expense, rather than in a common grave as had been originally intended. He also personally paid large compensations to the families of the victims.

But despite this, the impression that remained was of the dancing and festivities of the rich while thousands of poor people lay dying. The Tsar's many enemies, from radicals to revolutionaries, all pointed to the Coronation as a symbol of the uncaring nature of the monarch and his 'German woman'.

Shortly after his Coronation, Nicholas embarked on a foreign tour, commemorated above. *An early port-of-call was Balmoral in 1896, where the Royal couple enjoyed the company of the Prince of Wales and other members of the Royal Family* right. *Queen Victoria, distracted by the delights of her baby granddaughter, Olga, could not be persuaded to join the gathering for this picture*

TSAR AND TSARINA

After the Coronation, Nicholas and Alexandra enjoyed a pleasant and relaxing stay with relatives, before embarking on a European tour. In the summer of 1896, they visited Vienna, Germany and Denmark, where Nicholas's grandparents lived, and then sailed to England to pay their respects to the ageing Queen Victoria.

Finally, and most memorably, they visited Paris, to cement the treaty of alliance that had been signed in 1894, the year of Alexander III's death. There, they were given a flamboyant reception. The spectacle of huge crowds lining the great boulevards and chanting *'Vive L'Empereur'* impressed Nicholas deeply – an impression that was to strengthen the *entente* between the two great nations of such contrasting political systems.

Jean-Loup Charmet

A predictable routine

From the day of his accession until the outbreak of the Great War in 1914, Nicholas's day was divided up according to strict, unvarying rules. Breakfast was followed by interviews with ministers; afterwards there was always a short walk around the gardens; then audiences and guests for luncheon. After that, a drive with his wife, more work until tea, and afterwards, more meetings with ministers until 8 pm, followed invariably by a social engagement.

Sometimes in the evening the Tsar would take his wife on a sleigh ride far out on the 'Islands', a favourite promenade in St Petersburg. The rapid pace of the horses, the crisp snow flying under their feet, the quiet snowy Russian winter landscape – all were delights to them both. Alexandra loved her husband passionately, even fanatically, and such moments of intimacy were everything to her.

Early happiness

Right from the beginning of their marriage, Alexandra's life centred on her husband. Her days were arranged to seize any chance moment that the Tsar could give her. Always bright and cheerful, she was true to her childhood nickname of 'Sunny', the name by which Nicholas nearly always called her. Increasingly, she came to appreciate her husband's innate chivalry, his restrained temperament and great sense of duty. More and more too, she began to realize that, however conscientiously he set about his work, he was, by temperament and inclination, unsuited for the massive role of a supreme autocratic ruler that had been so prematurely thrust upon him. But in the early years of their marriage, she never sought to interfere with his political work, preferring instead to make a real home for her beloved husband and children.

Early in their marriage, Alexandra set about renovating and redecorating the Winter Palace and their living quarters at Tsarskoye Selo, where Nicholas had been born and had spent much of his childhood. Alexandra's tastes were deeply subjective, and her personality inevitably shone through her domestic arrangements. The walls of the private suites were lovingly hung with a discerning collection of paintings, and the tables were full of exquisite china and crystal. Yet Alexandra was not solely a collector of antiques. Above all, she wanted these rooms to be comfortable, exuding a homely atmosphere of children and dogs, rather than a cold museum.

Blissfully happy in their domestic life, Nicholas and Alexandra had three more baby daughters in four years. Tatiana was born in June 1897, followed by Marie in 1899. In June 1901 came their fourth child, also a girl, christened Anastasia.

🖾 *The Tsar's visit to Paris in 1896 set the seal on the newly formed Franco-Russian alliance. The significance of the occasion was not lost on the crowds, who gave him a rapturous welcome*

🖾 *In June 1901, Alexandra celebrated the birth of her fourth child, the Grand Duchess Anastasia*

By gracious permission of HM the Queen

THE WINTER PALACE

Once called the Venice of the North, St Petersburg was conceived as a new city by Peter the Great in 1703. On the bank of the River Neva, which runs through the city, he built the fabulous Winter Palace. Later, Catherine the Great brought in Italian architects who added the famous Hermitage to house her personal art collection. After the deaths of Nicholas and Alexandra, the city was finally renamed Leningrad. The Hermitage became a museum and the Palace remains as a lonely monument to a bygone age

Novosti Press Agency

Lavishly decorated in gold and white with crimson brocade drapery and panelling, this opulent boudoir was redecorated in the 19th-century for Empress Marie, the mother of Nicholas II. The strikingly patterned floor is of delicately inlaid wood

Victor Kolnev/Robert Harding Picture Library

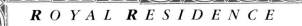

♕ A vivid green mineral, malachite, was used for all the decorations in the Malachite Drawing Room *left and below left*, which was used by the former Empresses. The decorative bowl in the centre is supported by winged figures in gilded bronze

♕ The painting *below* dating from 1881 shows the study used by Alexander II. Decorated in 19th-century style, the walls, desk, tables and even the doors are covered with family portraits. Sadly, these furnishings no longer exist

Bridgeman Art Library

♔ The Military Gallery *left* celebrated Russia's victory against the French in 1812. Paintings of 332 generals line the walls, together with portraits of Alexander I and his Prussian and Austrian allies

♔ The Small White Dining Room *right* was planned for family meals – the only colour comes from the tapestries on the walls. A musical box is hidden inside the revolving chandelier

♔ The dazzling Jordan Staircase *below*, with its Carrara marble balustrades and polished granite columns, was used by the Tsar on 6 January each year for the ceremony of the blessing of the waters of the River Neva

All interior photographs: Victor Kennett/Robert Harding

SHADOWS OF DARKNESS

John Massey Stewart

DESPITE THE TSAR AND TSARINA'S OUTWARD OPULENCE, GLOOM WAS DRAWING IN ON ALL SIDES. THERE WERE STRIKES, MILITARY DEFEATS AND ASSASSINATION ATTEMPTS – AND THE CHARISMATIC FIGURE OF RASPUTIN APPEARED ON THE SCENE

NICHOLAS WAS CONTENT IN HIS DOMESTIC life, but his problems as leader of the Russian Empire were enormous. Soon after his accession, he had made it clear that he would continue the policies of his father, and he dismissed as 'senseless dreams' a deputation of *Zemstvo* – popular council – delegates for daring to suggest that they might participate in governing the country.

Surrounded by many irresponsible favourites, including his three powerful uncles who often attempted to bully him, Nicholas was presented with a distorted picture of Russian life. Unfortunately, he distrusted many of his better advisers, fearing the loss of his sovereign powers.

Yet, through all his political troubles, Nicholas's view of his role as Tsar remained almost childishly simple. He had been elected by God, and only God could remove him. All who opposed him or sought to influence him to become more liberal, he suspected of being devilish conspirators. The problem was that Nicholas was forever trying to be something he was not. A naturally gentle and somewhat indecisive man, he was entirely without the qualities required to be a tough and tyrannical ruler.

Eventually, the uncertainties and indecisions of his reign resulted in Russia's humiliating naval defeat at the hands of the Japanese in 1904. Nicholas was confronted with a growing revolutionary movement which came to a head in a wave of strikes, demonstrations, riots, and massacres of Jews throughout Russia in 1905. He reacted by giving orders to suppress the uprising, using the hated secret police, the *Okhrana*, and

'My poor Nicky's cross is a heavy one to bear, all the more as he has nobody on whom he can thoroughly rely'

ALEXANDRA

the full force of military power at his disposal. Perhaps the worst example of this short-sighted policy occurred in January 1905, when a demonstration of peaceful, unarmed protesters led by a radical priest, Father Gapon, went to the Winter Palace to deliver a petition to the Tsar. They were met by sabre-wielding Cossacks on horseback. This cruel event, known as 'Bloody Sunday', reinforced the feeling of the Russian people that the Tsar was not their protector, as they hoped, but rather their uncaring enemy.

In spite of such alarming scenes, both at home and abroad, one ray of sunshine was allowed to enter the lives of Nicholas and Alexandra. On 12 August 1904, the longed-for son and heir to the throne of Russia, the Tsarevich Alexis Nicolaievich, was born. This child was the answer to so many heartfelt prayers. Alexandra had waited for him for so long that her overwhelming joy was clear to all who saw this outwardly reserved woman pouring out her soul in intense prayer in church. Nicholas wrote in his diary: 'A great, never-to-be-forgotten day, when the mercy of God has visited us so clearly.'

For Nicholas, the birth of this 'sunbeam' almost went so far as to outweigh in his mind all his political setbacks. The baby's christening at the Peterhof Palace on 24 August 1904 was like a pageant, and King George V of England (then Prince of Wales) was among the illustrious godparents. No heir to the crown had been born in Russia since the 17th century, and the ceremony was surrounded with a splendour to match its importance.

Hulton-Deutsch Collection

♛ *The birth of a son and heir, the Tsarevich Alexis, in 1904 brought great joy to the Romanov household. But that joy soon gave way to deep anxiety when Alexis was diagnosed as a haemophiliac. His childhood was dogged by a series of health crises that more than once took him to the brink of death*

Harlingue-Viollet

♔ Shipshape aboard the royal yacht Standart – *Nicholas, Alexandra and* from left to right *Olga, Alexis, Anastasia, Marie and Tatiana. This elegant steamship took the Imperial Family on their last visit to Britain in 1909*

Hulton-Deutsch Collection

♔ *Nicholas and Alexis centre at Cowes in 1909 with the future George V and his son Edward*

Popperfoto

♔ *Olga and Nicholas take the oars on a family boating trip, as Tatiana and Alexandra look on*

♔ *The Tsarina watches as her youngest daughter takes a riding lesson from her sisters Olga and Marie*

Hulton-Deutsch Collection

Popperfoto

♔ *Alexis, the four-year-old heir to the Romanov throne, dressed in traditional costume*

Popperfoto

♔ *Tatiana and Olga pose for the camera in full regimental uniform*

Popperfoto

♛ *Tatiana, in wistful mood before attending a royal gala*

Hulton-Deutsch Collection

Mansell Collection

♛ *Anastasia decides not to pause for the camera as she works at her knitting*

♛ *1914: caught in concentration – Marie, Tatiana, Anastasia and Olga*

Bildarchiv Preussischer Kulturbesitz

♛ *Alexis, taking his duties seriously, stands in uniform with Papa, 1916*

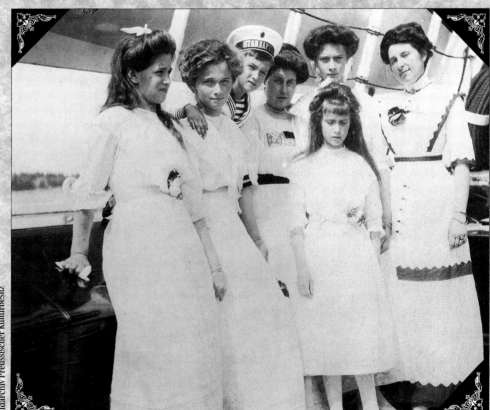

♛ *On board ship, the children pose with Alexandra's friend Anna Vyrubova centre*

DAWN OF A REVOLUTION

Alexis, the baby Tsarevich, was appointed honorary colonel of many regiments, and military decorations were showered upon his young head. As a public sign of his joy, Nicholas ordered amnesties of political prisoners and made large donations to various charities.

At his baptism, old Princess Galitzine, who had lived through the reign of many Tsars, carried the baby in her arms. So terrified was she of falling over that she had rubber soles fixed to her shoes so that she would not slip on the marble floor.

Shattering blow

Lying on a golden pillow, the baby was covered by a gold cloth lined with ermine, and cried loudly when old Father Yanisheff, the family priest, dipped him into the font.

According to Russian custom, the parents were not present at the baptism itself, but his small sisters, in short Court dresses, gazed open-eyed and somewhat nervously at the ceremony lest the elderly priest drop the precious parcel in the font. Olga, now aged nine, was given the privilege of becoming a godmother.

Six weeks after the christening, Alexandra noticed blood seeping from the baby's navel. The next day the bleeding stopped, but his parents' fears had been aroused. When he was a year old, Alexis started crawling about independently, but after the occasional tumble, his mother noticed large bumps and bruises appear on his arms and legs.

In deadly terror, but without speaking of it to anyone, Alexandra watched her darling with a fear in her heart that she dared not put into words. As the child grew older and more active, he developed typical swellings that pointed to haemophilia, the then incurable, untreatable blood disease. One of Alexandra's uncles had suffered from it and Alexandra realized that her only son, her beloved 'Sunbeam', had the same terrible condition.

In Nicholas's heart all the battleships lost at the hands of the Japanese, all the strikes, revolts and attempted assassinations could not compare with the cruel blow dealt him through the painwracked body of his little boy.

For years, this gentle and loving family man had desperately sought to be a strong and decisive monarch. But it was proving impossible to carry the burden alone, and more and more he found himself turning to his wife for support.

She had the strength of character and the sheer willpower that he lacked, and when it came to making tough decisions, he fell completely under her influence.

In 1906, urged on by Alexandra, Nicholas took back all the concessions he had made to a free parliament. From that moment, no matter how great the opposition he faced, Alexandra never allowed him to forget that he, and he alone, was the supreme ruler of Russia.

But the couple had other troubles. At first, they had clung to the hope that their son's haemophilia was only a mild form of the disease. But the boy fell ill again. Because the condition had been passed down to her son through her, Alexandra felt forever burdened by a terrible sense of responsibility. The look of deep and inconsolable sadness that would come over her now settled on her forever.

For the sake of the boy's future, and the future of the monarchy, the parents decided to hide their tragic secret from the world. The nature of the Tsarevich's complaint was unknown to almost all of Russia. Rumours flew: he was born defective, he was no longer alive; but no-one knew for certain what was going on inside the walls of the Imperial Palace. More and more, Nicholas and Alexandra withdrew into a world of their own.

Alexis's condition worsens

In 1912, Russia celebrated the centenary of the defeat of Napoleon's armies at Moscow. As part of the celebrations, the Imperial Family paid a hunting trip to Poland. During this visit, the Tsarevich Alexis, then aged eight, injured himself while jumping out of a boat. Internal haemorrhaging heralded the most dangerous attack he was ever to suffer, and a further fall caused a bad relapse.

Mary Evans Picture Library

Bilderdienst Süddeutscher Verlag

🕮 *The* Duma, *Russia's first elected parliament* below, *was a grudging concession to those who called for change*

John Massey Stewart

THE SEEDS OF REVOLT

The year 1905 was a turning point in Russian history, the beginning of the end of the people's belief in the Tsar. Humiliating naval defeat by little Japan sparked waves of unrest throughout the country. The large and good-natured crowds that marched on the Winter Palace in St Petersburg on 22 January 1905, singing 'God Save the Tsar' as they went, still had faith that Nicholas would listen to their grievances.

Their brutal and bloody suppression by massed ranks of Cossacks and Hussars *left and below* shattered the legendary belief that the Tsar and his people were one – 'The Tsar will not help us!' shrieked the marchers on that fateful day that became known as 'Bloody Sunday'. In a public statement, the priest who led them, the saintly Father Gapon, denounced Nicholas as the 'soul murderer of the Russian empire'. 'The innocent blood of workers, their wives and children lies forever between you and the Russian people,' he wrote. 'May all the blood which must be spilled fall on you, you hangman!' The Tsar himself, who had not even been in St Petersburg, was stunned by what had happened. 'Lord, how painful and sad this is!' he wrote.

'Bloody Sunday' was only the beginning of a year of unprecedented terror and violence, political assassinations, mutinies and riots

Mary Evans Picture Library

👑 *The Tsar's ministers had called for 'a small victorious war'. Yet the Japanese navy succeeded in taming the might of Russia. Ignominious defeat cost the lives of thousands. Political cartoons suggest a rapidly deteriorating image of the Tsar and Russia*

Jean-Loup Charmet

Mary Evans Picture Library

👑 *Nicholas hands out sacred images to troops bound for the Far East war with Japan. Alexandra made clothing and bandages for the casualties*

Bildarchiv Süddeutscher Verlag

At first, the little boy cried loudly and continually, 'Mama, help me.' In his earlier attacks, Alexandra, whose interest in hospitals had taught her the techniques of a skilled nurse, managed to soothe him and ease his pain. But now, she was powerless, and so were the doctors. 'When I am dead, it will not hurt any more, will it?' Alexis would ask his helpless mother. As his strength gave out, his cries became a constant wailing which grew hoarser and hoarser, his great eyes like sunken coals in his wan, drawn face. In the evenings, Alexandra would sit with him, stroking his forehead and pressing his hands. Nicholas would pace up and down, his face haggard with anxiety.

Miraculous recovery

It was at this stage that Alexandra turned in despair to a wandering faith healer and holy man, Gregory Rasputin. There had always been a mystical side to Alexandra's nature, and often in the past she had sought the advice of spiritualists and clairvoyants. Rasputin was summoned to the Palace and he prayed by the bedside.

It seemed to Alexandra that there was an improvement in the boy when Rasputin came, yet the doctors had told her that there was nothing more that could be done. Rasputin's message was consoling – the boy would not die. And, indeed, the next day, Alexis was better and continued to recuperate. The doctors pronounced him out of danger and, although he was to have further attacks later, Alexandra was convinced she had witnessed a miracle.

Problems crowded in on the Empress at this time. The glittering balls she attended angered the masses, even though they were social obligations that she herself might have wished to avoid.

High society

Every evening, at a succession of balls, banquets and receptions, stunning dresses and fabulous jewels would be paraded against the imposing setting of the Winter Palace. Young officers wore beautiful uniforms – every regiment of guards had a special 'gala' uniform. At Grand Balls, the Imperial servants wore special gold and scarlet liveries. Even the pages wore expensive feathered headgear, while the celebrated black ushers at the Winter Palace – one of them an American called Jim Hercules – wore oriental costumes, lending a touch of the exotic East.

At a Grand Ball, the entrance of the Imperial couple would be heralded by the master of ceremonies tapping an ivory-topped cane with the Imperial eagle embossed in gold. The ball would then open with a stately dance – the polonaise – which, by Court tradition, the

Mary Evans Picture Library

Jean-Loup Charmet

NICOLAS II LE PACIFICATEUR

Nicholas maintained good diplomatic relations with his cousin, Kaiser Wilhelm II of Germany top, although his political image elsewhere was coming under constant scrutiny above. And the conspicuous extravagance of the Grand Balls at the Winter Palace did little to help his and the Tsarina's standing with the ordinary people

👑 *The Tsarevich wears the uniform of 'Hetman of the Cossacks', the title he had borne since birth*

Popperfoto

Tsar and his wife would be expected to lead.

At the smaller concert balls (attended by some 800 revellers), the high point would be supper under the palms in the conservatory of the Winter Palace. These sumptuous feasts became famous throughout the world for their superb cuisine.

Yet, for all the opulence and outward gaiety of these functions, neither Nicholas nor Alexandra relished the obligations of the St Petersburg season. Nicholas, shy and timid by nature, tended to shun close contacts with his subjects and seemed to be able to relax only in the intimacy of his close family circle.

Alexandra was also a naturally shy person. At Grand Balls, when up to 2000 people were invited and she was expected to be introduced to half of them in an evening, she often found herself wishing the ground would swallow her up. Often her awkward Russian would falter, and she would blush deeply and look ill at ease. Coming to the position of Empress at such a young age, she had not had time to build up an intimate circle of friends to support and protect her during the rigours of social duty. There was no opportunity to get to know anyone better at official functions and, at the Court of the Tsar, where everything that happened was ordered by unalterable

tradition, there was little opportunity for more informal gatherings. St Petersburg society never really got to know Alexandra. Instead, her timidity was ascribed to haughtiness, her reserve to pride. Matters were not helped by what people saw as a sense of prudishness on Alexandra's part. Scandalized by the flaunted love affairs of St Petersburg society, Alexandra crossed more and more names off the Palace invitation lists – which served only to add to the antagonism against her.

Sadly, despite her considerable work for charity, particularly her patronage of hospitals, the Tsarina Alexandra never achieved a popular following among the Russian people.

Jean-Loup Charmet

RASPUTIN – THE HOLY DEVIL

With his hypnotic stare, Gregory Rasputin was a compelling – some said sinister – figure. Born of peasant stock in Siberia in 1872, as a young man he gained a considerable reputation as a drinker and womanizer. He was, nevertheless, said to have been blessed with extraordinary powers. Rasputin's arrival in St Petersburg as a holy man, or *staretz*, lionized by female admirers, was to have profound consequences for the ill-fated Romanovs

Popperfoto

EVERLASTING LOVE

The work of the Russian court jeweller, Peter Carl Fabergé, has lasted far beyond the Romanovs for whom his exquisite creations were designed. These and other intimate mementoes of the Tsar and Tsarina hold up a mirror to an age which disappeared dramatically in 1917

Wartski's/Forbes Magazine Collection

Wartski's

Wartski's/Weidenfeld Archives

Novosti Press Agency

👑 A delicate gold bracelet *above* features a flat-surfaced 'portrait' diamond surrounded by smaller precious stones. Some of the Imperial Family china *left* was made in 1807 and used for State occasions. The crystal was imported from England

Victor Kennet/Robert Harding Associates

👑 For this lovely gift box Fabergé used gold enamel decorated with the Imperial Russian eagle and the cipher of Nicholas II. The cigarette box *below*, with twin portraits of Nicholas and Alexandra, was made by Fabergé to mark the tercentenary of the Romanov dynasty

Victoria & Albert Museum

👑 The rose enamel egg *main picture*, with jewelled lilies of the valley, was given by Nicholas to his mother in 1898. Portraits of Nicholas, Olga and Tatiana spring out of the top

👑 The commemorative egg *top left*, decorated with miniatures of notable events, was given by Nicholas to Alexandra on their 15th wedding anniversary

👑 The Coronation egg *left*, given to Alexandra in 1897, has a replica of the Coronation coach inside

👑 Alexandra's jewelled opera glasses *below*, also by Fabergé

Wartski's

Edimedia

George Gibbes

George Gibbes

Popperfoto

From The Collection of George Gibbes

Hulton-Deutsch Collection

Nowosti Press Agency

♛ Like all young ladies of their generation, the Russian Grand Duchesses were expected to excel in the arts. Their watercolours *above* are a charming record of their travels throughout Russia. The traditional carved wooden house *left* was greatly loved by the Royal children

♛ A letter from Nicholas to his mother *left* inquiring after her health – they always remained in close touch, despite her differences with Alexandra. The beautiful tea service *below* belonged to Alexandra and was used for the quieter moments of domestic life that she cherished

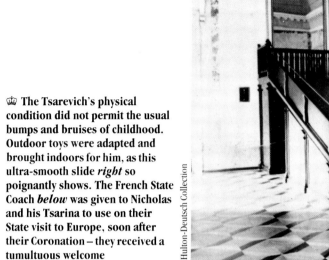

♛ The Tsarevich's physical condition did not permit the usual bumps and bruises of childhood. Outdoor toys were adapted and brought indoors for him, as this ultra-smooth slide *right* so poignantly shows. The French State Coach *below* was given to Nicholas and his Tsarina to use on their State visit to Europe, soon after their Coronation – they received a tumultuous welcome

Hulton–Deutsch Collection

Giraudon/Musée de la Voiture et du Tourisme

John Massey Stewart

END OF A DYNASTY

AS THEIR WORLD SPUN OUT OF CONTROL IN A STORM OF WAR AND REVOLUTION, NICHOLAS AND ALEXANDRA HAD JUST ONE CONSTANT TO CLING TO – THEIR EVERLASTING LOVE FOR EACH OTHER AND THE CHILDREN

 A relaxing boat ride on the River Dnieper in 1916. By this time the pressures on the Tsar were growing. The war was going badly for Russia and Alexandra's interference in affairs of state caused disquiet and anger

Marvin Lyons

THE CHARISMATIC RASPUTIN STIRRED STRONG feelings in St Petersburg society. Although he had many devotees, including the Empress Alexandra, who swore by his miraculous powers, he also had enemies who believed his influence to be sinister and corrupting. By 1912, all this attention had gone to his head and he began to abuse the power he held over his more gullible followers.

Tales of his lasciviousness and drunkenness swept St Petersburg. But from the start, one devotee refused to listen. In Alexandra's eyes, the uncouth peasant with thick dirty hair, powerful staring eyes, and a liking for liquor could do no wrong, and when rumours against him were re-

ported to her, she put them down to jealousy and class prejudice. Increasingly, she turned to him for advice and guidance.

The appearance of such a figure in the inner circle of the Imperial Family caused a great stir. Rasputin even kept his gruff speech and manner when he was with the Royal couple and spoke as informally to them as he would to commoners. There was a rumour that he had some strange influence over them.

One man who dared to speak out about Rasputin's influence was Nicholas's Prime Minister, Peter Stolypin. He was that rarity, an able statesman who was also completely loyal to the monarchy. But he had become alarmed by the clearly

scandalous hold that Rasputin had over the Royal Family and, for this, he incurred the displeasure of the Empress. At first, Nicholas hesitated to act against his Prime Minister, but gradually he yielded to Alexandra's pressure, and Stolypin was dismissed.

To many, it seemed that Russia was being governed not by Nicholas and his ministers but by his 'scheming' wife, aided and abetted by the 'evil' Rasputin. Alexandra had always appeared too aloof and reserved to become popular with the Russian people. Now, she was becoming hated, and there were wild and malicious – and quite untrue – rumours that she was Rasputin's mistress, and that her daughters were being brought up in immoral ways. Nothing, of course, could have been further from the truth.

War breaks out

The outbreak of the Great War in 1914 temporarily strengthened Nicholas's position, as Russians responded to the patriotic call to defend the motherland against Germany. But Nicholas did little to maintain this confidence. Patriotic organizations were thwarted in their efforts, the new parliament, the *Duma*, was slighted, and the gulf between the people and the Imperial Family grew. The situation worsened when Alexandra turned Nicholas's mind against his cousin the Grand Duke Nicholas, the popular commander-in-chief of the armed forces. Fearing a threat to the position of her revered and beloved husband and blinded by unswerving devotion, Alexandra's own judgements had become increasingly uncertain.

Worst of all, the armed forces were faring badly at the Front. The Germans had inflicted several humiliating blows on them, and on 5 March 1915, against the advice of his army chiefs, Nicholas dismissed the Grand Duke, assumed supreme military command and went to the Front himself.

Hulton-Deutsch Collection

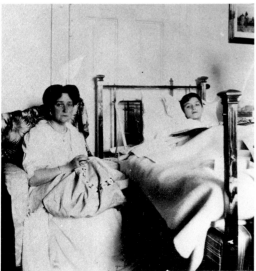

Roger-Viollet

♕ **Above** *Enthusiastic Moscow crowds greeted the Tsar and Tsarina during celebrations to mark the 1913 tercentenary of the Romanov dynasty. These celebrations were an opportunity to unite the Russian people behind the throne – 'We need merely to show ourselves and at once their hearts are ours,' said Alexandra. The sickly Tsarevich, Alexis, is carried by a Cossack bodyguard. Alexandra* left *nursed the haemophiliac boy devotedly*

In his absence from St Petersburg, supreme power passed, with Nicholas's encouragement, to the Tsarina, the only person on earth he trusted completely. In the midst of a desperate war, Russians watched horrified as Alexandra dismissed competent officers and replaced them with worthless nominees of Rasputin. Eventually, in December 1916, a group of nobles led by Prince Yussoupov decided to act. Poisoned with cyanide, shot in the head and body, Rasputin finally died by drowning after being pushed through a hole in the ice of a frozen river.

Alexandra, who was shattered by news of the assassination, never gave up her faith in the saintliness of 'our friend', as the Royal Family always called Rasputin. In return, she became an object of hatred and suspicion throughout Russia, dismissed contemptuously as 'the German

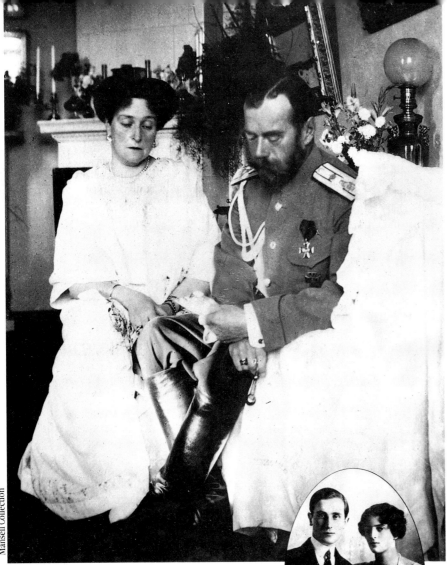

Mansell Collection

woman' and suspected by many of being a spy for Russia's greatest enemy.

Few cared to look at 'the other side' of Alexandra, the caring and sympathetic human being who, at the outbreak of hostilities, had set up a hospital for the war wounded at Tsarskoye Selo and who, despite her own ailing health, worked long hours as a field nurse in the army and Red Cross medical units. To her enemies, such obvious patriotic devotion to her fellow citizens meant nothing. Although Alexandra herself refused to contemplate it – in fact, she never did accept it – the fall of the Tsar was imminent.

Call to abdicate

On 5 March 1917, Nicholas sent from the Front what was to be his final telegram to Alexandra: 'In thought I am always with you and the children. God bless you. Sleep well. I kiss you tenderly.'

Three days later, serious riots broke out in St Petersburg (by now called Petrograd). Nicholas sent orders to the troops in the city to crush the revolt. But it was too late. Instead, the soldiers joined the uprising, and both they and the new representative assembly called on Nicholas to abdicate.

On 15 March, with great dignity, Nicholas renounced the throne – at first in favour of his son, but then, realizing that the sick child must be spared such an ordeal, in favour of his brother. 'I

🕀 *The Tsarina was convinced of Rasputin's powers – even when only reassured of Alexis's recovery by telegram* top. *Other members of the Royal Family, like his assassin Prince Yussoupov* centre, *thought him dangerous. Alexandra went into mourning* right *over Rasputin's death*

trust you will understand the feelings of a father,' he wrote to his new masters. Nicholas's brother Michael, however, refused the crown.

All through these tense days, Alexandra was without news of her husband. At Tsarskoye Selo, she could scarcely master her anxiety. The Emperor usually answered her telegrams in a matter of hours. Now there was total silence, and it became clear to her that the Revolution had spread beyond Petrograd and had reached the troops at the Front.

On the evening of 13 March 1917, the Tsarskoye Selo garrison itself, which until then had refused to join the rebels, left the barracks and marched out, firing haphazardly into the air. Hearing the news, Alexandra threw a black fur coat over her white nurse's uniform and went out into the snowy palace courtyard to rally the Palace Guard.

Walking from man to man, Alexandra told them that she had complete confidence in them, and urged them to remember that the life of the young Tsarevich – the heir of Russia – was in their hands. She even asked them, stiff with cold as they were, to come into the palace to warm themselves. The move seemed to work – temporarily, at least.

Inside the palace, the night was passed in great anxiety, despite the great number of now

Popperfoto

Mansell Collection

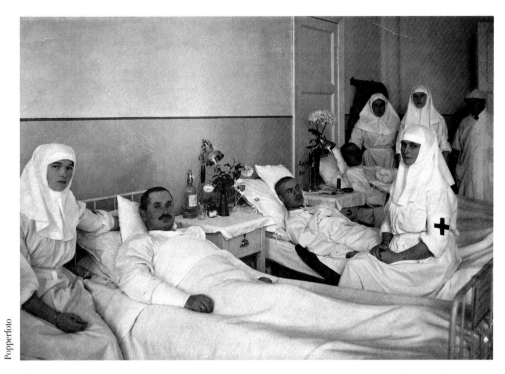

loyal guards outside. Alexandra had received a report that an armoured train manned by rebel soldiers from Petrograd was moving towards the Imperial station at Tsarskoye Selo. It was rumoured that the revolutionaries were anxious to get their hands on the Tsarina and her son, to hold them hostage in case the tide of favour turned against them. Other rumours said that they had sworn to murder her. Whatever their intentions, on reaching the actual village of Tsarskoye Selo, they became distracted and ran amok. Thoroughly and drunkenly aroused, several of them then set off for the Alexander Palace, where the Tsarina and her family were staying.

At the last minute, tragedy was averted, however. The rebels eventually withdrew because of reports that immense forces were massed to protect the Royal Family.

During the war years nursing became a passion with Alexandra. Here, she proudly wears the red cross of the qualified war nurse. Daughters Olga left and Tatiana standing, in the middle helped tend the wounded from the Front

Nicholas and Alexis enjoy an all-too-rare moment of private relaxation on a family holiday before the arrest

THE GREAT WAR

Optimism at the outbreak of war soon gave way to disillusion and anger as Russia suffered horrendous casualties on the Eastern Front and its army went into retreat. In 1915, the Tsar decided it was time to replace his distant cousin, Grand Duke Nicholas *left,* as head of the military – 'I shall assume command of the fighting forces, share the burdens and toils of war with my army and help it to protect Russian soil against the onslaught of the foe,' he explained. But his appeals for sacrifice were satirized and in Moscow street mobs called for the Grand Duke to be made Emperor in his place. Nicholas's new duties included troop inspections

THE INEVITABLE REVOLUTION

'To prevent a catastrophe, the Tsar himself must be removed, by terrorist methods if there is no other way,' said Alexander Kerensky in February 1917. The painting *below*, entitled *27 February 1917* and the work of a contemporary artist, depicts Petrograd in the grip of simmering unrest, the intense cold notwithstanding. Workers milled on the streets listening to revolutionary speeches, while soldiers watched and waited. Within a month, workers and soldiers had joined together to take over the seats of power and Kerensky was installed as leader of the provisional government

State Tretyakov Gallery, Moscow

DEATH OF THE ROMANOVS

On 21 March 1917, the day before Nicholas was at last expected to rejoin his family, Alexandra was officially placed under arrest by the new provisional government headed by Alexander Kerensky.

Alexandra now had the hard task of explaining to the children what had happened. They took the news as bravely as their mother had, and did their best to cheer Alexandra by speaking with joy of the one scrap of happy news – their dear father's return the next day.

Sombre return

On a cold and grey morning in March 1917, Nicholas, no longer Emperor, returned to his birthplace, the palace at Tsarskoye, where his family were now being held as virtual prisoners.

His car was stopped at the gates. 'Who goes there?', was the challenge. One of the soldiers answered, 'It is Nicholas Romanov.' After some negotiation, the car was allowed to drive up to the palace entrance. By their deliberate indifference and lack of respect, the soldiers showed how they now intended to treat their former sovereign.

Nicholas got out and crossed the great hall of the palace. Mechanically, he saluted the score of officers who watched him curiously. Very few of them returned his salute. Then Nicholas went at

Popperfoto

Poppertoto

Bildarchiv Preussischer kulturbesitz

once to his children's rooms where Alexandra was waiting to meet him. Their relief at finding each other alive, their pleasure in each other's company, were the only consolations they had.

The family were now prisoners in their own home. During the first weeks at Tsarskoye, Nicholas was allowed to go out for short daily walks, accompanied by soldiers with fixed bayonets. But he preferred to exercise by shovelling snow, rather than walk around and around in the limited space that was offered him.

Alexandra did not go out at all. She and the children spent each day in their rooms. The evenings they spent together were filled with unspeakable sadness.

Royal prisoners

Nicholas's treatment at the hands of his revolutionary jailers grew steadily worse. Every time he ventured out, he was insulted to his face, baited and humiliated. On one occasion, when he took a bicycle ride in the gardens, a soldier deliberately stuck his bayonet in the spokes of the wheels, causing the former Emperor of Russia to fall helplessly in the snow while all around laughed at his plight. Through all this, Alexandra lost weight rapidly, aged noticeably, and sat for hours on end in almost total silence.

Meanwhile, as the revolution in Moscow and

♛ In March 1917, as the tide of Bolsheviks swept the country, the Imperial Family were under house arrest at Tobolsk in Siberia. Constantly under guard, Nicholas maintained his dignity and pride throughout his captivity above. His children were treated with great respect by the locals – they are shown left sitting on the roof of a house that served as their prison – and relaxing for a moment outside top right. Cartoons became progressively more contemptuous. Lenin is shown below sweeping the old order away

Тов. Ленин ОЧИЩАЕТ землю от нечисти.

Petrograd was taking its unpredictable course, no-one seemed sure what to do with the Imperial Family. There had been talk of Nicholas being put on trial. Then the provisional government planned that he and his family should be allowed to find exile in England. But instead, mainly due to the opposition of the Petrograd revolutionary workers' and soldiers' council – the power base of Lenin, Trotsky and the Bolshevik Party – the family were moved from Tsarskoye to Tobolsk, in Siberia, where their treatment improved somewhat. Many local people felt a sentimental loyalty to the Tsar and attempts were made to make their detention as reasonably comfortable as possible. Alexandra spent her days lying on the sofa and knitting, while Nicholas would read aloud to his children.

In October 1917, Lenin took over the reins of power. The advent of Communism sealed the family's doom. In 1918, they moved to Ekaterinburg (now Sverdlovsk) in the Urals. When the anti-Bolshevik 'Whites' approached the area, the local Communists were ordered to prevent a rescue.

The decision was made to execute the Royal Family and to destroy all evidence of the deed. Nicholas suspected that a change of plan was in the air. Although Alexandra had been tired and ill, he and the children had remained in relatively good spirits. Now Nicholas grew tense and watchful.

On the evening of 16 July 1918, the leader of the secret police guarding the Royal Family, Jacob Yurovsky, told his men, 'Tonight we will shoot the whole family, everybody.' The family went to bed as usual. At midnight, Yurovsky wakened them, explaining that the 'Whites' were approaching and that they must be moved at once. Innocent of the fate that awaited them, the family dressed and went downstairs, where Yurovsky led them to a basement room and told them to wait for their cars to arrive.

Into this small room crowded Nicholas and Alexandra and their five children, and four mem-

bers of their domestic household, including Alexandra's parlourmaid, Demidova, who carried some Imperial jewels hidden in the feathers of a pillow. As they settled down to wait, Yurovsky burst into the room waving his revolver, followed by his armed secret policemen. 'Your relations have tried to save you. They have failed and we must now shoot you,' Yurovsky declared to the terrified group.

In the hands of God

Nicholas hardly had time to throw a protective arm round his wife before Yurovsky pointed his revolver at the Tsar's head and fired. Nicholas died instantly. The secret police then opened fire, and the small room rang with shots and screams. Alexandra was making the sign of the cross when she fell dead, hit by a single bullet. The Grand Duchesses Olga, Tatiana and Marie also fell in the hail of bullets. The sickly Tsarevich was finished off by two bullets through the ear.

The Grand Duchess Anastasia, who had fainted when the firing started, now regained consciousness, and was set upon by bayonets and rifle butts. The Romanov dynasty – and with it, Tsarism – was at an end.

'I have a firm, an absolute conviction that the fate of Russia – that my own fate and that of my family – is in the hands of God,' wrote Nicholas. He was to die as a martyr to circumstance, but the tragedy – and triumph – of Nicholas and Alexandra lie in their undimmed courage, and the supreme love that sustained them in their final days.

⚜ *Tsar Nicholas, clutching the Tsarevich Alexis, is executed by his Bolshevik captors at Ekaterinburg – but is this what really happened? Mystery and intrigue still surround the final days of the Romanovs*

Jean-Loup Charmet

Hulton-Deutsch Collection

From the collection of George Gibbes

MYSTERIOUS POSTSCRIPT

To this day, there are those that believe that the Romanovs did not perish on that terrible night at Ekaterinburg, that they were kept alive by their captors and then managed to escape.

The most intense speculation surrounds the fate of the Grand Duchess Anastasia *left*. Books and plays, and a film *Anastasia*, starring Ingrid Bergman, have taken as their subject Anastasia's survival and flight, and two different women have come forward claiming to be the Tsar's surviving youngest daughter. The most plausible of these 'Anastasias' is Anna Anderson *inset*, who was rescued from a Berlin river in 1920 after a suicide attempt. Throughout her life, she has never wavered from her story that she and the Grand Duchess are one and the same person.

Anna Anderson's claim has never been disproved, though neither has it ever been officially accepted